Facing the Final Foe

James E. Carter

BROADMAN PRESS
Nashville, Tennessee

© Copyright 1986 ● Broadman Press
All rights reserved
4254-33
ISBN: 0-8054-5433-0
Dewey Decimal Classification: 242.4
Subject Headings: CONSOLATION // DEATH
Library of Congress Catalog Card Number: 85-19517
Printed in the United States of America

Library of Congress Cataloging-in-Publication Data

Carter, James E., 1935-
  Facing the final foe.

  1. Death—Religious aspects—Christianity.
2. Bereavement—Religious aspects—Christianity.
3. Consolation. I. Title.
BT825.C386 1986   248.4'86106   85-19517
ISBN 0-8054-5433-0

To the memory of my grandparents,
B. A. and Ellie Martin Reaves and
T. A. and Molly Moseley Carter
from whom I early learned
to appreciate life and
first learned to face death

Preface

Death is an inevitability.

No family escapes the pain of death. No person escapes the threat of death. In 1 Corinthians 15:26 the apostle Paul asserted that "the last enemy that will be abolished is death" (NASB).

If death is, indeed, our final foe, how can we face the final foe? How can we react, and even survive, when we have faced the final foe through the death of one dear to us?

This book is designed to give aid, assurance, comfort, strength, help, and hope to those who have faced the final foe through the death of a loved one. In this purpose, I trust that God will use it to help each one of us in this experience shared by all of us.

Part I is a brief study of death itself from a biblical perspective.

Part II deals with the questions that confront us at the death of someone whom we love.

Part III contains some words that are designed to encourage and support when death has occurred. These focus on the Christian faith and the biblical truths in an attempt to help individuals in a difficult time.

Part IV focuses on some of the times along life's journey when death invades our lives. We should try to find positive, helpful ways of dealing with that experience at those times.

The material in this book has been developed over more than thirty years of pastoral ministry. Some of the concepts were found in an earlier book I wrote entitled *What Is to Come?* published by Broadman Press. They were also expressed in "Life After Death," a learning module published by the Church Training Department of The Sunday School Board of the Southern Baptist Convention. Many people and the churches with whom I have been privileged to serve also contributed to the book.

At the time the book was in preparation, I was teaching a class in pastoral ministry at Southwestern Baptist Theological Seminary as an adjunct professor. Some of the ideas were tried out on those students. I am grateful for their response.

The typescript was prepared by Pat Bohanan, pastor's secretary at the University Baptist Church, Fort Worth, Texas, who left the position before it was completed, and Jo Dominy, who assumed that role. I am grateful for their help.

I am also grateful to the University Baptist Church, Fort Worth, Texas, where I am privileged to serve as pastor, for their response to my ministry in this area and to my wife, Carole, for her continued encouragement for my writing.

I trust that the Lord will be able to use the book to help you as you face the final foe.

Contents

PART I
A Word About Death

1
When Death Comes

Philip of Macedon, the father of Alexander the Great, had a slave to whom he gave a standing order. The man was to come to the king each morning of his life, and, no matter what the king was doing, he was to say to him in a loud voice: "Philip, remember that thou must die."

Death is a certainty. Someone has said that the only sure things in life are death and taxes. There could conceivably be a way that one could escape paying taxes. There is no way that anyone can escape death.

Death is a natural consequence of life. All things that live must also die. Human experience has shown us that all people must die. Perhaps Elijah and Enoch could be considered exceptions, but they also departed this life. Life is composed of change. And death is a change from life as we know it to another kind of life.

Death is the cessation of life as we know it. Medical advances have caused a closer examination of the biological meaning of death. When does life actually cease? Does it cease when the brain stops functioning? Does it cease when the body stops functioning normally? Does it cease when the person no longer responds to stimuli?

When death comes, the Christian does not deny death. Neither, however, would the Christian glorify it. Christians face death; they do not fear death.

The Bible realistically faces the fact of death. In the Bible people died. The certainty of death in human life is neither ignored nor deemphasized. It is realistically faced. Death comes to all people, even Bible people, even Christian people.

Jesus really died. His death on the cross was not just a dramatic act. It was an actual fact. When Jesus Christ tasted life as we live it, He also experienced death as we know it.

We, too, must realistically face the fact of death. We could wish it otherwise. But the fact of life and human experience remains: death comes. And that fact we must realistically face.

We try to postpone death. In any hospital, battles are waged all day each day to try to postpone the inevitable fact of death. The medical profession is pledged to sustain life as long as possible. And that is good. But death with dignity has become an issue in our day. Through mechanical means and by advanced medical technology, people have been kept alive for days or weeks. All we can ever do with death is to postpone it, we never escape it. Death ultimately occurs.

Then when death comes, we try to camouflage it. When we look upon the body of a loved one at the funeral home, we say, "Doesn't she look natural." We never say, "Doesn't she look dead." Many of our funeral practices are attempts to camouflage death. The setting in which the service is held, the preparation of the body, and the practices of shielding the family are all attempts to cover up the fact that we stand in the presence of death.

Then we try to ignore it. We say, "He passed away." We usually do not say, "He died." But die we do. Death will eventually come to all of us.

While the Christian faces death, the Christian does not fear death. The reason is that Jesus Christ has made even the experience of death a new experience. The One who sat upon the throne in the Book of Revelation proclaimed, "Behold, I make all things new" (Rev. 21:5). And that includes death itself.

Jesus brought about the death of death. Listen to these words of assurance from the apostle Paul:

> For this perishable nature must put on the imperishable, and this mortal must put on immortality. When the perishable puts on the imperishable, and the mortal puts on immortality, then shall come to pass the saying that is written: "Death is swallowed up in victory." "O death, where is thy victory? O death, where is thy sting?" The sting of death is sin, and the power of sin is the law. But thanks be to God, who gives us the victory through our Lord Jesus Christ (1 Cor. 15:53-57).

When death comes it is *an* end but not *the* end. Death is an end to life as we know it, an end to earthly relationships that we enjoy, an end to the service that we render to God here on the earth. But it is not the end of all life. It is not the end of all existence. God has given us life, and God is with us in life, and God is with us in death.

Even though we know this, death always comes to us as an invader. We call death "the grim reaper" because we consider death so final. We are not certain of what lies beyond.

For the Christian, death does not come as an enemy. It opens the way for a greater life with God. D. T. Niles has been quoted as saying that death is not an end but an exit, not a blank wall but an open door.

At times, death actually comes as a friend. In the case of an individual who has lived a long, useful, and fruitful life, death at a full age may come as a friend. When there is a terminal illness from which one cannot possibly recover, death may come as a friend.

Death may come at an early age, at old age, after a lengthy illness, or from an unexpected accident. But death does come to all of us. And Christ is with all of us—in life and in death.

2
What Death Is

Two boys, about five and seven years of age, were at the graveside services for their great-grandmother. Others had left the graveside to speak to friends. But they stood there as the casket was lowered into the grave and the grave was filled. As the casket was lowered, one of them said to the other, "There she goes. Look she is going down." Then as the clods of dirt fell on the casket, they counted the shovelfuls of dirt until they were dragged from the scene by their mother. They did not avoid the obvious fact that one had died and had been buried.

Adults are not often that open in the face of death. Even though we are aware that all persons must die at some time, we are self-conscious and uneasy in the presence of death. It seems to be such a mystery to us. What is death, anyway?

Death, the cessation of life as we know it, is a change. It is a change from one kind of existence to another kind of existence.

Life is the gift of God. The creation account tells us, "Then the Lord God formed man of dust from the ground, and breathed into his nostrils the breath of life; and man became a living being" (Gen. 2:7). And the psalmist added, "For with thee is the fountain of life; in thy light do we see light" (Ps. 36:9).

The continuation of life is dependent upon God. As God gave life to us as a gift He sustains life for us. The prophet Isaiah showed the contrast between those in the place of the death and the living in their praise of God for the life that God had given. Listen: "For Sheol cannot thank thee, death cannot praise thee;/those who go down to the pit cannot hope for thy faithfulness./The living, the living, he thanks thee, as I do this day;/the father makes known to the children thy faithfulness" (Isa. 38:18-19). The life that has been given by God returns to God at death. As the Preacher expressed it in Ecclesiastes, "The dust returns to the earth as it was,/ and the spirit returns to God who gave it" (Eccl. 12:7). Thus, the Bible does not teach of the innate immortality of the soul. All life is dependent upon God. Life itself is a gift of God.

The Old Testament people feared death. *Sheol* was the abode of the dead without respect for the character of the dead. It contrasted with the land of the living in every respect. In death there was thought to be a cessation of conscious communion with God and service to Him. That is expressed in Psalm 6:5 where the psalmist asked, "For in death there is no remembrance of thee;/ in Sheol who can give thee praise?" A dead body was considered unclean. The Old Testament gives some intimations of resurrection but does not fully develop a doctrine of resurrection (see Isa. 25:8; 26:19; Dan. 12:2).

Death is related to sin. Death came into the world because human beings chose to sin. Notice how Paul expressed it: "Therefore as sin came into the world through one man and death through sin, and so death spread to all men because all men sinned" (Rom. 5:12). This does not mean that an individual's death is caused by his or her sin, but that humankind tastes death because of sin. Death is one of the consequences of the entrance of sin into the world.

With the coming of Christ, even the concept of death is made new. Jesus referred to death as sleep. When Jesus arrived at the home of Jairus whose daughter had died, He said, "Why do you make a tumult and weep? The child is not dead but sleeping" (Mark 5:39). And when He learned of the death of His friend Lazarus He said to His disciples, "Our friend Lazarus has fallen asleep, but I go to awake him out of sleep" (John 11:11). Death was something which brought quiet and rest rather than something to be feared. In the story of the rich man and Lazarus, Jesus assured us that life does not end with death. The body is consigned to the ground, but the life, the self, goes on. To Jesus death was secondary to life in the will of God. He showed that when a man volunteered for discipleship (Matt. 8:21-22).

By His death and resurrection, Jesus defeated death. Sin and death are the greatest human problems. These were both conquered by the death and resurrection of Jesus. By regeneration and resurrection, they can be defeated in the life of the believer in Christ. At the time of the death of Lazarus of Bethany, the brother of Mary and Martha, Jesus gave reassurance to Martha when he told her, "Whoever lives and believes in me shall never die" (John 11:26). The apostle Paul asserted that our Savior Jesus Christ "abolished death and brought life and immortality to light through the gospel" (2 Tim. 1:10).

God has given us life, and God is with us in death. Albert M. Casteel was a missionary who died with cancer. About nine months prior to his death, he wrote an article entitled "As I Face Death" in which he stated that life is the greatest miracle. He asked how this brief pilgrimage could be compared with eternity. Since Christians think in terms of eternity they do not concern themselves too much with the brevity of life, whether it is forty years or eighty years. In death, as in life, Christians live with God.

The change brought about by death can be compared with birth. There is life both before and after birth; but it is life in a different sphere, a different kind of life. The Christian continues to have life after death, but it is a different kind of life. Leslie Weatherhead wrote in *The Christian Agnostic* that death is a mere milestone, not the end of the journey. He believed that people pass on into another phase of being, to another class in God's school.

What is death? Death is the cessation of life as we know it and a change in existence. When death comes, life on this earth ceases; but life with God continues. Through faith in Christ, the Christian is delivered from death and given life through Christ. John the Seer proclaimed, "Blessed are the dead who die in the Lord" (Rev. 14:13).

3
What Death Does

In a sermon included in his biography, *A Man Called Peter,* Peter Marshall told of a little boy, an only son, who was incurably ill. Month after month his mother had tenderly nursed him, read to him, and played with him, hoping to keep him from realizing the dreadful finality of the doctor's diagnosis.

But as the weeks went on and he grew no better, the little fellow gradually began to understand that he would never be like the other boys he saw playing outside his window. As small as he was, he began to understand the meaning of the term *death* and he, too, knew that he was to die.

His mother had been reading to him the stirring tales of King Arthur and his knights of the Round Table. She read of Lancelot and Guinevere, and Elaine, the lily maid of Astolat, and of that last glorious battle in which so many of the fair knights met their death.

As she closed the book one day, the boy sat silent for a while as though deeply stirred with the trumpet call of the old English tale. Then he asked the question that had been weighing on his childish heart: "Mother, what is it like to die? Mother, does it hurt?"

Quick tears sprang to her eyes, and she fled to the kitchen, supposedly to tend to something on the stove. She knew it was a question of deep significance. She knew it must be answered satisfactorily. So she leaned for an instant against the kitchen cabinet, her knuckles pressed white against the smooth surface, and breathed a hurried prayer that the Lord would keep her from breaking down before the boy and would tell her how to answer him.

And the Lord did tell her. Immediately she knew how to explain it to him.

"Kenneth," she said as she returned to the next room, "you remember when you were a tiny boy how you used to play so hard all day that when night came you would be too tired even to undress and you would tumble into mother's bed and fall asleep?" That was not your bed. It was not where you belonged. And you would only stay there a little while. In the morning, much to your surprise, you would wake up and find yourself in your own bed in your own room. You were there because some-one had loved you and taken care of you. Your father had come and, with big strong arms, had carried you away. Kenneth, death is like that. We just wake up some morning to find ourselves in the other room —our own room where we belong—be-cause the Lord Jesus loved us."

The lad's shining, trusting face looking up into hers told her that the point had gone home. There would be no more fear, only love and trust in his little heart as he went to meet the Father in heaven. He never questioned again. And several weeks later he fell asleep, just as she had said.

Through death we are allowed to pass from this kind of existence to another, from this place to another place.

At the time of a loved one's death, we concentrate upon what we have lost. We have lost a companion. We have lost a mother or father or sister or brother or husband or wife or son or daughter or friend. We have lost the good times, the shared experiences, the relationships with that person. The loss is real. The pain is real. The grief is genuine.

But we may also want to think about what that person had gained. He or she has gained a fuller life, an entrance into the very presence of the Lord. He or she has gained the opportunity to miss the sorrows, the disappointments, the hurts, and the misfortunes of this world. He or she has gained a freedom from pain and disability. And freedom from the fear of death.

Death is not a defeat. It is a necessary prelude to entering into the new kind of existence with God. Consider the death of Jesus, for instance. When He was on the cross, His enemies taunted Him and jeered at Him. He was defeated they felt. But then three days later, He arose from the dead and spelled the end to the power of death over persons. Death was not His defeat but the prelude to victory.

Death is this kind of change for the Christian. Rather than saying in the hour of death, "We lost the battle; she has died," there may be times when we can say, "Now she has gone to be with Christ. She has experienced a change that opens the door to greater life."

Just before His own death, at a time when one would think that Jesus would be morose, sad, or defeated, He attempted to prepare His followers for His death. These are the words of victory rather than defeat:

> Let not your hearts be troubled; believe in God, believe also in me. In my Father's house are many rooms; if it were not so, would I have told you that I go to prepare a place for you? And when I go and prepare a place for you, I will come again and will take you to myself, that where I am you may be also (John 14:1-3).

The Christian does not have to fear death. Jesus has delivered the believer from the fear of death. The writer of Hebrews said of Jesus, "He himself likewise partook of the same nature, that through death he might destroy him who has the power of death, that is, the devil, and deliver all those who through fear of death were subject to lifelong bondage" (Heb. 2:14-15). A new power, the power of the Holy Spirit, has come into the life of the Christian.

Death is the last enemy to be faced. But through Christ, it is not only faced but also defeated. Through death the entrance into a larger life of continued fellowship with God is made possible. Hear Paul, the apostle, "For we know that if the earthly tent we live in is destroyed, we have a building from God, a house not made with hands, eternal in the heavens. He who has prepared us for this very thing is God, who has given us the Spirit as a guarantee" (2 Cor. 5:1, 5).

Death opens up eternity and blessedness for us.

4
What Death Cannot Do

In a eulogy presented at the funeral service of actress Gracie Allen, George Jessel said that the hope of mankind must be in the faith that the play is never over—when the curtain falls, it rises again. He went on to state that if we did not believe this, then it has all been a big gag and the punch line is futility.

This expresses the hope that all people have that life does not just end at death. For Christians, this goes beyond hope and becomes an assurance.

We are very much aware of what death does: It brings to an end the earthly life of one with whom we have shared life; it separates us from those whom we love; it robs us of the fellowship, the love, the life experiences with our loved ones. What death does we know. But what is it that death cannot do?

Death cannot separate us from the love of God in Christ Jesus. Listen to the assurance expressed by Paul, the apostle:

> Who shall separate us from the love of Christ? Shall tribulation, or distress, or persecution, or famine, or nakedness, or peril, or sword? As it is written, "For thy sake we are being killed all the day long;/ we are regarded as sheep to be slaugh-

tered." No, in all these things we are more than conquerors through him who loved us. For I am sure that neither death, nor life, nor angels, nor principalities, nor things present, nor things to come, nor powers, nor height, nor depth, nor anything else in all creation, will be able to separate us from the love of God in Christ Jesus our Lord (Rom. 8:35-39).

Notice in the list of scary possibilities that Paul listed death as the very first thing that could not separate us from the love of Christ. In fact, Paul indicated that we are superconquerors over death ("more than conquerors"). In another place, Paul indicated that the last enemy Christ would destroy is death (1 Cor. 15:26). But here he assures us that through Christ this final foe has not only been faced but defeated.

The power of death over human beings has been defeated by Christ (1 Cor. 15:21, 56-57). Because Jesus has been resurrected from the dead, so will all believers be resurrected also. Jesus once asked Martha, the sister of Lazarus whom Jesus raised from the dead, a searching question: "I am the resurrection and the life; he who believes in me . . . shall never die. Do you believe this?" (John 11:25-26). And Paul posed the rhetorical questions to death itself, " 'O death, where is thy victory?/O death, where is thy sting?' The sting of death is sin, and the power of sin is the law. But thanks be to God, who gives us the victory through our Lord Jesus Christ" (1 Cor. 15:55-57).

Many people believe in some form of survival, that something remains that is still that person even after death. The belief in some form of survival can be Christian or non-Christian. The ancient Greek philosophers believed in immortality, the concept that there was something in a human being that could not die, a spark of the immortal. Christians believe in the resurrection. Resurrection centers in the power of God to raise from the dead.

Though one has really died, God's power gives life. We have the assurance of resurrection through the resurrection of Jesus Christ from the dead. Paul described Christ's resurrection as "the first fruits of them that slept" (1 Cor. 15:20, KJV). The firstfruits are the first grain or fruit that is harvested. They are the promise of more to follow. Christ's resurrection is the promise that Christians will be resurrected also.

The passage read often at the graveside gives the assurance of the resurrection of those who believe in Christ.

> But we would not have you ignorant, brethren, concerning those who are asleep, that you may not grieve as others do who have no hope. For since we believe that Jesus died and rose again, even so, through Jesus, God will bring with him those who have fallen asleep. For this we declare to you by the word of the Lord, that we who are alive, who are left until the coming of the Lord, shall not precede those who have fallen asleep. For the Lord himself will descend from heaven with a cry of command, with the archan-

gel's call, and with the sound of the trumpet of God. And the dead in Christ will rise first; then we who are alive, who are left, shall be caught up together with them in the clouds to meet the Lord in the air; and so we shall always be with the Lord. Therefore comfort one another with these words (1 Thess. 4:13-18).

For the Christian, death can be a victory. So much can be overcome in death. The limitations, the infirmities, the deformities are all gone. Where we have served so ineffectively and limitedly up to then, death removes these barriers; and we can be ushered into the very presence of God to serve Him directly and without the barriers of time, space, and flesh.

This emphasis is a challenge to us. Because of what we know about death and the resurrection of the body, because we know that life has not ended but is still going on, because we know that what is done in this life will live and continue forever, we can work more faithfully for Christ. We can be steadfast. We can be unmovable. We can always continue in the work of the Lord. We can comfort one another with these words. All of this is because we know assuredly that our labor and our lives are not in vain.

The resurrection of Jesus from the dead and the resurrection of the Christian from the dead stand together. Because Jesus was resurrected from the dead, we have the promise that we also will be resurrected to live with Him eternally.

What is it that death cannot do? Death cannot separate us from the love of God. We believe in the resurrection of the body. We are not souls that exist in some shapeless state. We are persons who live in a continued relationship with God that goes on because, through God's power, we go on.

PART II
A Word at Death

5
Why Have a Funeral Service?

She was a lovely and talented nineteen year old. A childhood friend of my son, she suffered from a form of cancer. They had been a part of a select group of young people who had begun an expanded program in the laboratory school of a state university. The group had developed strong ties and close friendships. She was hospitalized for most of the fall semester in a major hospital in a large city in an adjoining state. My son was attending a university in that state. That fall, he spent most weekends visiting with her and her family. At her funeral service, he served as a pallbearer.

At the cemetery following her interment, he asked, "Why do we have to do this? Why do we have to go through all of this?" Why, indeed? Why have a funeral service?

That thought may have occurred to you also. Why have a funeral service? Is there not a simpler and easier and less traumatic way to bring a life to a close? Actually, the funeral service performs a valid service to the family and friends of a deceased person.

The funeral service performs a rite of *closure*. In a specific way, the family and friends are able to say good-bye to the person with whom they have shared life. They face up to the reality that this chapter of life has been closed. They accept the fact that this person has actually ended life as we know it.

I know a young lady who was serving as a short-term missionary in Korea when her grandmother died. She was not able to attend the funeral. After she returned home, she indicated that it took her a long time to realize that her grandmother was actually dead. A funeral service helps that process along. It is a way of closing out the life of that person.

We have a number of other rites of passage in our culture. We acknowledge in certain ways that a person has reached a certain age, has attained a certain position, or has accomplished a certain goal. Sometimes they are recognized by a ceremony as baptism or graduation. Other times they are celebrated with a party as a birthday and usually the birthdays that mark decades are especially significant. A funeral service marks the rite of closure. It helps to acknowledge the end of the earthly life.

A funeral service also aids in *coping* with the fact of death. This allows a person to admit that the loved one or friend has actually died. We have strange ways of denying facts many times. With the presence of the body before us, in the company of friends, and with the assurances of the Christian faith ringing in our ears and finding ways into our hearts, we can admit it: She has died.

One of the ways that we cope is through the expression of grief. Grief must be ex-

pressed. It will express itself in one way or
another. In some way, grief will work itself
out in the human life. The funeral service is
a socially acceptable way for an individual
to express the grief that is felt at the loss of
a loved one or friend. That grief can be
expressed at the funeral service without em-
barrassment or apology.

There, also, you are surrounded by loving family and concerned, helpful friends.
You draw strength and courage from the
strength and love they share with you at
that time. It helps to know that you do not
face that hour of grief, loss, and pain alone.

Through the funeral service when the
truths of the Christian faith are shared and
the hope that we have in Christ is enunciat-
ed, we become aware of a spiritual strength.
It is then that we can follow the biblical
suggestion, "Cast all your anxieties on him,
for he cares about you" (1 Pct. 5:7). Then
we remember the word of the psalmist,
"Cast your burden on the Lord, and he will
sustain you" (Ps. 55:22). The assurance
that the Savior Himself gave us in His last
words also take on new meaning, "lo, I am
with you alway, even unto the end" (Matt.
28:20, KJV).

A funeral service is also a time of *celebra-
tion.*

We can celebrate the life of the individual. Each human life has something to com-
mend it. Each individual had someone to
whom he/she was very important. Each
person gave and received love. At the funeral service that person's life can be celebrat-

ed. Even the fact of life itself which is made more dear and is understood more clearly as a gift of God in the presence of death and is understood.

We are aware that the life of each one of us is diminished to a degree when someone with whom we have shared life dies. John Donne's words remind us that no man is an island and that anyone's death diminishes each of us. Therefore, he said, "Never send to know for whom the bell tolls; it tolls for thee." At the funeral service, we celebrate life itself and particularly the life of the deceased.

We celebrate the hope and the assurances of the Christian faith at the funeral service. At that time, we are reminded of the truth of the resurrection, of the power of God's love, and of the assurances of eternal life. The Christian hope becomes very real.

Christian faith and hope are being celebrated at the funeral service and suggest something of the nature of the service. Hope is positive, not negative. Hope has a bright side, not a negative note. Hope brings peace and assurance, not morbidity and doubt. The Christian funeral service can celebrate that hope positively, brightly, and with assurance.

The funeral service has a practical purpose and a real value in human lives at the death of a friend or loved one. Use it positively. Make it a time of strength and help.

6
What Kind of Funeral Service Should It Be?

He was one of those interesting characters who are recognized in small towns but are often lost in the crowds in a larger city. For most of his life, he had worked as a barber. But he also began lending money out of his hip pocket and in a few years had built up such a prosperous loan business that he abandoned the barber trade. He was a Methodist; his wife was a Baptist. So both the Methodist minister and I were participating in his funeral service when he died after a long bout of cardiac illness.

As we got together to plan the service, the Methodist minister shared with me one of the things the man had told him some time earlier. He had directed the minister to conduct his funeral service in such a way that the people would know who had died and was being memorialized. He did not want a general, generic funeral service. He wanted a personal, custom service. He had been a regular listener to our Sunday evening services that were broadcast over the radio each week. He always commended me when the sermon was taken from the Old Testament. So he also directed that primarily Old Testament Scriptures were to be used in the service.

What kind of funeral service should it be?

Each family faces those decisions whenever death occurs. Some people have already helped their families by making those decisions themselves. At our church, we have on file the funeral service plans for a number of our people. On occasion I have visited the family prior to the funeral to discover that the deceased had planned the service in detail, including the musical selections and the Scripture passages to be included.

Most ministers will consult with the family before planning the service to see that the Scripture passages that were meaningful to the deceased person or to the family are used in the service. They will also want to coordinate the musical selections with the family as closely as possible.

A number of questions always emerge in planning a funeral service.

The first question is, where shall it be?

Funeral homes have chapels where the service can be conducted. Obviously, it is less difficult for the funeral directors if the service is held in the funeral home rather than in the home or a church. They are already there. They are set up for the service. They do not have to move the body, flowers, or personnel to another place to conduct the service.

It is also often easier for the family to have the funeral service at a funeral home. Some people do not feel that they could worship later in the same spot where they had the memorial service for a loved one. They feel they would visualize the casket there and relive the service Sunday after Sunday. Having a funeral service in a funeral home does not make it any less Christian than having it in a church. It is the content of the service, not the place where the service is conducted, that makes a service Christian.

Many people prefer to have the funeral service in the church. This is particularly true if the deceased person has been very much a part of the church and the church has been a vital part of that person's life.

There is something positive to be said about conducting the memorial service in the context of Christian worship and in the place dedicated to the worship and praise of God. It sets the final farewell for the individual within the context of Christian witness.

Rarely are funeral services held in homes anymore, even though this is still the practice in some locales. People often object to this for the same reason that they would object to having the service in the church: They are afraid they could not erase the memory. However it does put the home going in the context of a natural and expected stage of life.

Next, who will conduct the service? If a person is related to a church, normally the pastor of the church will conduct the service. Other ministers who are meaningfully related to the family and other staff ministers in the church can surely assist in the service. Many funeral homes have organists and soloists, either on their staff or on call, who can help in the service at the funeral home.

What about the service itself? Here are some guidelines that may be helpful in planning the service.

Make it positive. The funeral service does not have to be morbid and depressing. There is grief, loss, and pain. These are usually present at every time of death. They should be dealt with and honestly faced. To play them up and to dwell on them is not necessary. The Christian faith has a positive note of hope in it. This should be emphasized.

Make the service personal. It is not necessary to make the whole service a eulogy. The service should be designed for that individual. A generic funeral service is not very comforting. The deceased was a person and had a personality. That should be recognized. Of course, it should be honest and true. Do not claim for the person more than he or she was. A mother once instructed her son during a funeral service to slip up and see if it were his father in the casket. The description did not sound like him.

Make the service Christian. In the Christian context, the service should emphasize the hope, the promises, the assurances of the Christian faith. A lot of Scripture should be used. The music should adequately express the beliefs. The power of the Holy Spirit and the promises of God should be brought to bear on the lives of the sorrowful.

Make the service helpful and strengthening. People need comfort and assurance at the funeral service. Those who remain need the strength to take up their lives and to continue living creatively. The strength brought by God helps them then.

Make the service brief. A long, drawn-out service is not necessary. A half hour for the service itself is usually adequate. There is a great deal of stress in many lives at the time. Some have traveled far to attend the service. It does not have to be long to be helpful and comforting.

The funeral service is a means of witness for Christ and affirming the Christian faith.

7
How Shall I
Tell the Children?

Our older son was three years old at the time. He had a dog, part Boston bull terrier and part something else, whose name was Indian. His pet turtle was named Indian, and he wanted to name the little brother he would soon have Indian, also. Indian the dog died. As dogs are wont to do, he got into the street, was struck by a truck, and died.

We prepared to tell our son about the death of his pet and, in the process, about death itself. In a very serious mood, the three of us sat on the couch in the living room. I told him, "Indian has been killed." His mother cried. My son asked, "Why?"

How will you tell the children about death? Their experience is so limited. Their spirit is so trusting. Their love for a parent, a grandparent, a brother or sister is so complete. Just how will you break the tragic news to them that one of these who meant so much to them has died?

Very carefully. You tell the children about death very carefully. Since so much of what they will understand and experience as children comes more from what they have sensed emotionally than from what they have been told verbally, you will

want to be careful how you tell children
about death.

You will not want to tell them about
death in such a way that they will fear death
all of their lives. Some adults can never face
or accept death because of the perceptions
of death that have remained with them
since childhood. The presentation of death
should not produce an irrational fear of
death nor a morbid curiosity about death.

Neither will you want to present death to
them in such a way that God is made to
seem more an enemy than a friend. When
a child is told that God took her parent, she
may look upon God as one who takes away
from her those people who are most meaningful and dear to her. The religious faith
that one has can greatly strengthen, encourage, and engender hope in the time of death.
But the presentation of death in a way that
makes God seem to be the one who deprives
and punishes people by removing the ones
they love most can create destructive atti-
tudes toward God.

Within the context of faith, death can be
presented to a child. For a child who has
been put to bed each night of his life with
a prayer to God who is his friend and helper
death can be related to the tender and loving God who is with us both by day and by
night. For a brother to go to be with that
Jesus who has been our Friend and Companion throughout all of life is a much more
comforting thought than to be told that
God always picks the prettiest flowers in
the garden. If that were true, the child may

wish that his brother had been ugly, mean, and untalented so that the brother could have lived to share life with him.

We need to have a healthy attitude toward death in order to tell the children about death. If death is threatening and frightening to us, that fear will be caught by the children. Very young children will catch the emotional climate much more than the meaning of the words that are expressed. Because of the children's limited experience they may not be able to understand the reason for the charged emotions but they can pick up the emotional climate.

This brings up the question, should a child be allowed to attend the funeral service? If the funeral service is conducted in such a way as to celebrate life and to affirm the power of God in human lives, the child could profit from sharing this experience with the family. He could very well understand that better than he could understand being separated from the family at a time that he is aware of the high emotional level of the family. On the other hand, if the service is conducted in a morbid, depressing manner that emphasizes deprivation, and perhaps the depression that has come to the family due to the loss by death, it could contribute to the warping of the child's concept of death. The love, acceptance, and strength of the family has a great deal to do with the answer to that question. The child cannot always be shielded from the fact of death. Death is a part of life. When death is experienced within the context of its naturalness, the family's love, and the Christian's faith, these can become the building blocks that help to construct a healthy and wholesome view of death.

A child should be told about death honestly. The questions the child asks should be answered as honestly and as fully as necessary. More information than the child desires or needs is not necessary. Adults often think they have to answer children's questions more fully than is really necessary. The child just wants an answer to that question, not a full dissertation on death. Remember that children, especially young children, are literal and concrete in their understanding. Abstract concepts are difficult for them to understand and process at early ages. Adults can interpret the child's natural curiosity as a morbid matter. When adults whom a child loves and trusts discuss death with the child with a minimum of anxiety, the child knows that it is all right to talk about the feelings that trouble him or her.

Keep in mind the developmental nature of childhood. All children are not at the same stage of development at the same age in life. And each age group has its own developmental stage. Up to three years of age, the child will have limited language facility. Generally that child will need to be reassured of love and closeness, that he or she has not been abandoned because a loved one has died. From about age four to nine, language facility has improved. Death may be related more to the biological meaning of death. The understanding of the finality of death is being formed. The questions need to be answered fully and honestly. From ten to the teens, children are beginning to realize that death is inevitable. They are even beginning to face the possibility of their own deaths. Death should be explained in ways that do not bring about guilt or anxiety for them.

Myron Madden in *Raise the Dead* talks about letting the biology of death correct the childish psychology of death. Death has no power that we do not give it. In discussing death with children, remove the horror of death and implant the beauty and meaning of life.

8
What's Good About Grief?

They thought she was the very picture of Christian strength and composure. At the funeral service for her twelve-year-old son who had died suddenly, she did not even shed a tear. She should have. Within a few months, she began to show signs of instability. Before the first anniversary of the boy's death, she had suffered a complete mental and emotional breakdown.

What's good about grief? Grief allows us to express our feelings of loss and pain. Grief permits us to admit and accept the death and separation of a loved one. Grief gives us the time to adjust to life without the loved one and to put together the life that must go on.

Grief will work itself out somehow. It would have been much better for the mother to have expressed the grief that she felt in her heart. Openly expressed grief can be dealt with constructively. The grief that is not expressed, that is repressed, that is not admitted, works itself out destructively. Grief is good when it allows the person to face up to the sorrow, to express the loss and grief resulting from it, and to constructively handle the emotional impact of death.

Grief usually proceeds through some

normal stages. The normal stages of grief do not always follow in the same order for each person or last the same period of time or occur with the same intensity. We are all individuals. As individuals, we respond to different things in different ways. But there are some elements of commonality that run through them all.

Several years ago Elisabeth Kübler-Ross made an extensive study of people facing death. The results of her study were published in a well-known and well-distributed book entitled *On Death and Dying.* She identified five stages through which people go as they become aware of a fatal disease and the termination of their own lives. These stages are: denial and isolation, anger, bargaining, depression, and acceptance. When one first knows that he will die he just denies it. Related to that is the isolation that the person experiences. He isolates himself from others, perhaps not even sharing his news; and he feels isolated from the world that goes on as though he is still in good health. Then anger. After that he attempts to bargain, perhaps with God, in an effort to buy more time. Depression sets in as he realizes he will not continue to share life with his loved ones or reach his life goals. Finally, there is acceptance. Many of these same stages, in some degree, can be found in the grief process of those whose loved ones have died or are dying.

Others have identified the normal stages of grief as shock; the feelings of distress, suffering, or agony; abnormal reactions to what is going on, as just sitting and staring into space or the inability to concentrate; guilt; and hostility.

What does one do when these normal stages of grief are experienced? They can be faced and dealt with destructively or constructively.

One destructive method of dealing with grief is withdrawal. A person may simply withdraw from the world around him. Not communicating with family or friends, refusing to engage in the normal methods of recreation or relaxation, often failing to eat or rest properly is withdrawal from the world. A short withdrawal time to regroup or to recover the balance after a grief experience is normal. To withdraw from the world and to build a shell around oneself, only leads to destructive consequences in the life.

Abnormal activity can also be a destructive way of dealing with the grief one feels. The unusually active person compensates for her loss by keeping so busy that she never has time to face what has happened or to deal with the grief. An endless round of engagements, activities, diversions, and compulsive working keep the individual from ever getting serious about the grief work that is necessary for healthy living.

What about the person who denies the death of a child, a parent, or a mate? An extreme case is the woman who kept the body of her mother secreted in her room for years. Or it is the mother who never changes or rearranges or updates the room of her boy who was killed by a speeding trucker when he was ten years of age. The room always looks as though he would come home from school again any minute, even though the accident occurred years before. Quite obviously no one wants to wipe out all memory or discard all mementos of a deceased loved one. But to deny that death and to act as though the person could reappear any moment is a destructive way to handle grief.

Grief can be handled constructively by realistically facing it. Certainly there is pain, loss, sorrow, and the feeling of deprivation. Death is real. Sorrow is genuine. It is not to be denied; it is to be faced. When the sorrow is faced, it can be handled. To have sorrow is not a sign of weakness. To admit sorrow and to begin the process of working through it is a sign of maturity.

Expressing grief is constructive. The ways of expressing grief are as varied as the people who experience grief. It may be through crying. Some people prefer to carry their grief alone and will seek solitude for awhile. Others want someone around them to share that time with them. Simply talking it out often helps. Do not despair if you realize that you have told the same story in the same sequence and in the same words to a dozen different people. Talking about it can be therapeutic for you.

Give your grief to God. The prophet recorded the directive of God, "Comfort, comfort my people, says your God" (Isa. 40:1). God gives us comfort. We can give our grief to God and find His strength in our time of sorrow.

Good grief! Grief helps us to face the realities of death and to renew the processes of life.

9
Where Is
He/She Now?

A few years ago a brilliant American theologian died at the untimely age of forty-six. Among those who mourned his death was a three-year-old boy who was a playmate of the theologian's little daughter. He felt perplexed and indignant over what had happened to Wendy's daddy. The little boy's mother told him that Wendy's daddy was with God. The lad replied in tones of acceptance and understanding, "Oh! Then he's still real!"

As Christians we have that assurance. When someone dies that person is still real. But if they are still real, where are they now? This question has haunted people for years. Believing that God both offers and gives eternal life, believing that death does not obliterate the person, believing that there is a resurrection of the dead, where is my loved one now? What do the dead do until the resurrection occurs?

Some unacceptable answers have been offered to that question. From both the biblical perspective and the standpoint of faith, some answers do not seem sufficient.

One such answer is soul sleep, the idea that at death a person enters into a sleep from which he or she does not awaken until the resurrection. The Bible does refer to death as sleep, but this is a metaphor to remove the fear of death.

Annihilation is the concept that at death the unbelieving person is simply annihilated. But this runs counter to the New Testament understanding that all people have some conscious life after death.

Some believe that a person's eternal destiny is not fixed at death, leaving open the possibility of cleansing between death and resurrection. This belief has been rejected by Protestant and Evangelical believers basically because of their understanding that a person's destiny is fixed at death.

Many of the Eastern religions believe in reincarnation, the belief that at death the soul is recycled to another life. Through a process of rebirths, a soul is cleansed of all moral evil. When it is clean enough, it is simply absorbed into some cosmic mind or order and loses self-consciousness. Others have adopted this view in some form. The personal, unique nature of each human being's life argues against this belief, as well as the understanding that our debt for sin has been paid through the death of Jesus Christ.

A belief in the transmigration of souls is similar to reincarnation. It also is the concept that human beings go through a series of lives (not always human, incidentally) in order to be cleansed of evil. Basically the same arguments against incarnation could be used against this idea.

Universalism, which is the belief that in the end all persons will be saved anyway, is sometimes suggested. These folk think that ultimately everyone will find themselves in a state of bliss and will enjoy the blessings of heaven. Universalism is rejected because of the beliefs that God is just, that sin is real, that the atonement of Christ has meaning, and that definite decision for Christ is demanded.

If these answers do not really answer our question of where our loved ones are now, what is the answer?

We can begin to get a glimpse of the answer when we look at the story of the rich man and Lazarus in Luke 16:19-31. Both of the men lived after death, though in very different places. Each had a conscious existence after death.

The teaching about life after death in this story is peripheral. The main teaching of the passage has to do with the fixing of destiny while in life. Destiny cannot be changed after death. It does tell us, however, something about the life beyond the grave.

We run into the problem of how to describe the life beyond the grave. Some would prefer to call it *an interim state,* others like to use the term of *an intermediate state,* while still others choose to call it *a disembodied state.* Some Christian thinkers have even suggested *an intermediate body* since Hebrew thought could hardly conceive of a life without a body. Whatever term is used it is the state between death and the resurrection—the present life of the dead.

Notice that it is a place. The rich man

was in a place identified as Father "Abraham's bosom" which to pious Jews would be a place of blessedness. However, the rich man's place was separated from blessedness. He was neither in the presence of the faithful nor in the presence of God.

What shall we call those places? *Paradise* could be a name for the place of righteousness. Jesus promised the thief on the cross, "Today you shall be with Me in Paradise" (Luke 23:43, NASB). It is a place of conscious existence with Christ. Those who are not Christians are in a place of conscious existence also, but it is separated from God. Any place separated from God is a place of anguish, anxiety, and unpleasantness. *Hadēs* is a biblical name. It translates the Hebrew word *sheol* which means simply the place of the dead.

The place is a fixed state. People could not go back and forth from one place to another. It was also an incomplete state. After death, there is a resurrection and a judgment, then a final destiny. Destiny is fixed at death, but it is not assigned until the judgment. So we feel that those who die go immediately to a place, a place either in the presence of God or separated from God.

In the presence of God, there is peace. And in the presence of God the promise of eternal life is realized. Job raised the haunting question, "If a man dies, will he live again?" (Job 14:14, NASB). Jesus Christ gave the answer, "I am the resurrection and the life; he who believes in Me shall live even if he dies" (John 11:25, NASB).

But it seems like a long time to us from death to resurrection. To the one who has been removed from the time and space references of life on this earth, it may seem but an instant. Remember that the Scripture tells us that "with the Lord one day is as a thousand years, and a thousand years as one day" (2 Pet. 3:8, NASB).

10
How Do We
Face the Fact?

My father died when I was thirty years of age. He had been ill for about eighteen months before his death. About a year prior to his death, my family and I had moved from a neighboring state to a city about seventy-five miles away from where my father lived. Since it was only an hour and a half's drive, I tried to spend as much time with him as I could during that year.

I remember quite vividly that a number of times after Dad's death I would think, "I must tell Dad about that, he would enjoy that," or "Dad can help me as I make this decision; he will know what I ought to do." Then I would realize: "I cannot tell Dad anything; I cannot ask Dad anything; he is dead." And I would be struck with an almost overwhelming wave of grief. It would seem for a moment like I had been hit by something. How do you accept the fact of the death of a loved one?

It is not always easy. The person who tells you that it is easy has not faced it realistically. There is also a sense in which a person who has not experienced the death of a parent, a mate, a child, a brother or a sister cannot actually know how it is. You can sympathize with another person, you can even emphathize with another person, but until you have experienced that loss yourself you cannot really know what it is like.

God does strengthen you. God's presence is comforting and encouraging. God's peace does stand guard over you. But another truth is that you must face, accept, and deal with the fact of death. I do not know how many times I had told other people about the "peace of God, which passes all understanding" (Phil. 4:7). What I had told them was true. But I did not know its real meaning and its full force until after the death of my father.

You begin to face the fact of death when you realistically accept the fact that your loved one has died. That is not always as easy as the statment sounds. He or she did not pass away or go away or leave; he or she *died*. And that fact must be faced.

Duke K. McCall retired as president of a seminary after many years of service. He also served a term as president of an international religious organization. After McCall's wife's death, he wrote an article entitled "My Wife Died" which was carried in many denominational papers. On Easter 1982, as it began to dawn, he stood by his wife's bedside in the hospital intensive care unit. After having read the Easter story aloud, he placed his hand on his son's shoulder and prayed. Without planning it, he prayed, "Even so, come quickly for her, Lord Jesus." His wife took a deep breath and died. His son commented that God had heard his father's prayer and had taken his mother home. McCall testified that death came not as an enemy but as a friend; for, he stated, death is not an end but an entrance, not a goal but a gateway.

But Duke McCall also advised people not to avoid talking about death. Death is the last enemy only for the non-Christian. For a Christian, "to die is gain." And he reminded us that the phrases used in place of *death* do not help. How he really felt about it just exploded from his heart when a well-intentioned acquaintance caught him off guard by saying that he was sorry that McCall had lost his wife. Before he could edit his remark, McCall replied that he did not lose his wife; he knew where she was; he was the one who was lost.

Facing your own sense of loss, pain, sorrow, and loneliness is also how you face the fact of death. You do not gain anything by denying those feelings or by delaying those emotions. They are real. They are normal. And they must be realistically faced. After the death of his wife, C.S. Lewis commented, in a book called *A Grief Observed,* that no one had ever told him that grief felt so much like fear. He said that he was not afraid but the sensation was like being afraid—the same fluttering in the stomach, the same restlessness, the yawning. And he kept on swallowing. Until the death of my father, I did not know that grief made you so tired physically. I remember the exhaustion I felt when we got home after the funeral.

As those emotions just mentioned are

processed, some other feelings must be dealt with as you face the fact of death. One is the matter of feeling relieved after the death of one who has suffered a lot and a long time. For that person, death may indeed have come as a friend rather than an enemy. Life as it had been known and enjoyed could never again be possible. To feel relieved that death has occurred is no reason for guilt. It is, instead, the realistic appraisal of the situation.

You should not feel guilty either that you are still alive and your loved one is dead. You may think that the person for whom you grieve had more to offer than you do, had more to live for than you do, and could contribute more to life and the world than you can. But all of that is beside the point. The fact is that person died and you still live. That is one of the mysteries of death: why death strikes one person and not another, why death comes at one age and not another, why death occurs in one situation and not in another. Death is a mystery that we cannot solve. To attempt to solve it is only to bring more confusion. We simply must accept the fact that we still live.

A glib expression of the will of God is not helpful. To tell the truth, we do not always know and understand the will of God. To explain some things by the will of God would make God appear something other than the God of love who saves, accepts, loves, and wants the best for all of His children. Using that expression may be an easy

way out rather than an accurate statement
and means of help in many cases.

Life must go on. You may not always
know how it will go on, but it must continue. Since you are still alive, you will accept
the fact of death, deal with your grief, and
live your life in the strength of God and
with purpose. You learn to live with your
grief. Your life is still meaningful.

PART III
A Word for Death

11
A Letter at Death

Dear Shane

I have delayed writing you following your father's death in order to get a little perspective on it. Even though we don't know one another well, I knew and loved Bob from the time he was a baby. I always felt very close to him, even when we weren't physically close as we have not been for several years now. When we were both much younger, I thought of him as the little brother I always wanted but never had.

I was thirteen when my Uncle Pete, Bob's father and your grandfather, died. His was the first death of anyone close to me, and I can still remember how it affected me. My mother, Sue Mamma, said that burying Bob was almost like burying Pete again. They looked so much alike, their ages at death were so close, and her love for both of them was so deep. I am sure I would have had some of the same feelings if I had been able to be at your father's funeral.

Death is certain. As sure as there is life, there is also death. Death comes to all things that live. So it is a bit strange that we treat something that is so certain like a stranger. But we all think we will never die. We all fail to deal with the fact that those closest and dearest to us will die. So death always comes as a stranger, an intruder. We are never ready for it; we are never prepared for it. This is even more true when the person who dies is young, the death is tragic, and it is totally unexpected—as in the case of Bob's death. You just have not had time to prepare yourself for it emotionally. It comes as a shock . . . and it leaves us in shock.

You can deal with death in several ways. As you work through your grief, all of these things come at one time or another, often not in any order.

You may try to deny death. You try to convince yourself that it did not happen, it was a mistake, or that it is a bad dream from which you will eventually wake up. I was in Arkansas when Uncle Pete died. He came by to see me at my Grandfather Carter's house when he left to go to Texarkana. So I had seen him just a few days before he died. The news hit me hard. I was there for the whole thing, funeral and all. For months after that, whenever I was in a crowd, I would search the faces of the people hoping that I would see Uncle Pete. I was hoping that it had all been wrong, hoping that somehow, somewhere he would show up again. But in the end, death is not to be denied. It is real. A funeral service helps you to say good-bye to the one you loved and lost.

You may get angry. Anger at death is a

natural reaction. Someone you loved and valued has been taken away from you and you are mad. That's OK as long as that response passes and you don't let it settle in to make you a bitter person. You can't go around carrying a grudge against God or your father or somebody you don't know so you get mad at the whole world.

You may try the road of resignation. That's to say, "Well it was going to happen anyway, sometime." Other people may encourage this. They sometimes tend to get smooth and syrupy and tell you some things that just aren't so. They may try to explain it by the will of God. God allows some things to happen because people are free and can make their own choices that are really not His will as far as what God wants for folk. God doesn't want a young man with promise and potential who is loved by a lot of people to die tragically. But He allows it to happen because we are people and not puppets; people can make choices and do things on their own and sometimes what they do is not all good. Neither is it right to just flippantly say that everything is going to be all right in the end. In the end, most people do get through these crises and come out all right on the other side; but it isn't easy or automatic. I learned that at your age. I was in the back bedroom with my grandmother who was resting on the bed exhausted and grief stricken at the death of your grandfather. One of our aunts came breezing in to say, "Now Ellie, everything's going to be all right." I had trouble buying that then, and I don't buy it now. You don't just resign yourself to it, and it works out fine. Some people have twisted the meaning of Romans 8:28. It doesn't mean that all things that happen are good. It does mean that God can work with us and salvage every situation so that we can gain some good from it—strength, faith, understanding, hope. I have always liked the way the Revised Standard Version translates that: "We know that in everything God works for good with those who love him, who are called according to his purpose." God can work in everything. And He does.

This brings you to the acceptance of death; you realistically accept the fact that death has occurred and that it is real. You work through your grief and come out on the other side always with a pain in your life but also with a gleam in your eye and faith in your heart. You face the fact that life goes on, that your life goes on, and you must make the very best of your life. And you place your faith in God in a wholesome, healthy faith that draws strength from Him each day and rests on the promises of the Christian faith.

You can have the assurance that you left Bob's body at the cemetery in the woods by the old field but that Bob has gone to the presence of the God who gave him life. You have the assurance that as Jesus Christ was resurrected from the dead so will those who believe in Him be resurrected to live with Him eternally. Death is an end but it is not *the* end, and you have the assurance that God will neither leave you alone nor comfortless. Jesus Himself promised, "Lo, I am with you alway, even unto the end" (Matt. 28:20, KJV).

Shane, you have lost something precious and valuable in the death of your father. But there are some things that even death cannot take away from you: your father's death cannot take away the life given to you by your father. His death cannot negate the love he had for you or that you had for him. His death cannot erase the memories that you will always carry with you. His death cannot remove the assurance you have of your father's faith in Christ. God doesn't let loose of those who have laid hold on Him. The special relationship you had with your father will always support you, even though you are not together physically.

Bob had not always had peace, now he has peace in his heart, rest in his soul, strength in his body, and assurance in his mind.

You will probably never know how your father died. So there will always be some uncertainties in your mind. But there are also some certainties that you will never want to lose: love, faith, hope, life. You have the challenge before you to live your life to the fullest, to realize your potential to the greatest, and to achieve your best because you had a father who loved you and was proud of you. The fact that he can't share in those achievements should encourage you to your best rather than discourage you from your best.

God bless you, Shane, in these days of acceptance and adjustment.

12
The Savior's
Suggestion for Sorrow

He was such a handsome child. He had played a rousing game of football the day before. During the night, a fever had come up. The infection was severe. His funeral was held three days later. How do you handle the sorrow that comes from that?

She was a beautiful, popular, and promising teenager. She was a passenger in the automobile that attempted to take the curve too fast. When the sheriff and the pastor told the family in the early hours of the morning, sorrow seemed to overwhelm them. How do you handle sorrow like that?

They had only been married a month when he was shipped overseas with his army outfit. She was a bride of less than a year when she became a widow. Her sorrow seemed more than she could bear. How do you handle sorrow like that?

Sorrow always comes to us somewhat as an invader. We have planned our lives and are pleased with our existence. Suddenly that is all shattered by the death of a loved one. The dominant emotion then becomes the sorrow. That death may come suddenly and unexpectedly as death comes before us as an enemy, or it may be after a long life and a lingering illness when death comes to us more as a friend. But death always brings sorrow with it no matter what the circumstances of its arrival.

Are there any suggestions for dealing with sorrow? Yes. Many people will offer suggestions. Any number of people will offer sympathy. Others will share comforting and consoling words. Food, flowers, and friendship will be offered to you in your sorrow.

But amid all these caring expressions, the Savior makes a suggestion for dealing with sorrow: "Peace I leave with you; My peace I give to you; not as the world gives, do I give to you. Let not your heart be troubled, nor let it be fearful" (John 14:27, NASB).

At a time when we would think that our hearts should be both troubled and fearful, the Savior gives to us a practical and positive word: "Let not your heart be troubled, nor let it be fearful."

The time when these words were spoken is significant. This section of John's Gospel is what is called "The Farewell Discourses." Jesus was preparing His disciples for life on the earth without His physical presence. To the human mind, the followers of Jesus had reason to have had troubled hearts and fearful minds. Jesus was staring death in the face. He had already predicted more than once to His disciples that He would be betrayed, tried, and crucified. The events were already under way in Jerusalem. The decision had already been reached: Jesus must die. So in the face of His own death, at a time when His closest followers would soon know sorrow, the

Savior gave a suggestion for dealing with sorrow.

Twice in chapter 14 (vv. 1 and 27), the Savior gave that reassurance: "Let not your heart be troubled." For that kind of reassuring and strengthening suggestion to be repeated, there had to be some basis for it. As we look at the Scripture passage more carefully, we can see the basis and understand why the Savior gave this suggestion for sorrow.

The Savior's suggestion for dealing with sorrow has a *reason*. The reason for the Savior's suggestion for sorrow is found in the peace that He gives. Notice that before Jesus ever suggested to the disciples that they have untroubled hearts and unfearful minds, He said, "Peace I leave with you; My peace I give unto you; not as the world gives, do I give to you" (14:27).

The sequence is important. Before we can know the untroubled hearts and the unfearful minds, we must have the peace of Christ. Jesus gives us His own kind of peace. That is obvious from the statement. Jesus' peace is different from the world's peace.

For the world, peace is negative. We think that we have peace when we do not have trouble. If there is no trouble, if there is no fear, if there is no fighting, then we are at peace. But Christ's peace is positive: in the middle of problems, there is peace; in the midst of sorrow, there is peace; in the experience of pain, there is peace.

The Savior's suggestion for dealing with

sorrow needs a *response*. Notice that Jesus tied in His suggestion of the untroubled heart and the unfearful mind with belief in God. He said, "Believe in God, believe also in me" (14:1).

The response of the trusting heart brings about the peace that Jesus gives. When we trust in Him, we have peace. When we live in obedient faith, we have peace. That does not mean that all of our questions are answered. We still will ask, Why? Jesus even asked from the cross, "My God, My God, why . . . ?" (Mark 15:34). But it does mean that, even with the questions, we have God and we know His peace. He never leaves us. He never forsakes us. He always cares for us. And He continually shares His peace with us.

The Savior's suggestion for dealing with sorrow faces *reality*. Jesus was always realistic with His followers. He made known to them the demands of discipleship. He let them know of His impending death. He prepared them for life on this earth without Him. Jesus was realistic.

The reality is that life continues even with the sorrow. Life goes on even though it will go on without someone with whom we have shared life, someone very dear to us. Since life goes on, we must learn to handle the sorrow, to face life, to make the life that remains as full and meaningful as possible. The disciples wouldn't have honored Christ if they had frozen life at the moment He died. Such a response from us does not honor our loved ones either.

The Savior's suggestion for dealing with
sorrow is that we know and experience His
peace. In place of troubled hearts and fearful minds, we can have strength in sorrow
through Christ's peace.

13
On Eagle's Wings

(*Note: This is a funeral sermon I preached for a friend.*)

The colonel was a flyer. He joined the United States Air Force to fly. So intent was he on flying that he was always reluctant to reveal that his college major was journalism; he was afraid they would make him a public information officer. And fly he did. He flew many kinds of aircraft to many places and on many missions. For almost thirty years, he flew. On eagles' wings, he flew in God's great sky.

Therefore, when we come to the memorial service for his life, we get great comfort from the concluding verses of the first chapter of the section of Isaiah's prophecy we call the Book of Comfort, Isaiah 40:27-31:

> Why sayest thou, O Jacob, and speakest,
> O Israel, My way is hid from the Lord, and my judgment is passed over from my God?
> Hast thou not known? hast thou not heard,
> that the everlasting God, the Lord, the Creator of the ends of the earth, fainteth not, neither is weary? there is no searching of his understanding.
> He giveth power to the faint; and to

them
that have no might he increaseth
   strength.
Even the youths shall faint and be
   weary,
and the young men shall utterly fall:
But they that wait upon the Lord shall
renew their strength; they shall mount
up with wings as eagles; they shall
run, and not be weary; and they shall
walk, and not faint (KJV).

Perplexed by events, the prophet pointed people to the greatness of God. God would not only renew their strength but would exchange strength with them. In exchange for their weakness, perplexity, and difficulty to understand in the face of circumstances, God would give His strength. One of the results would be that they would "mount up with wings as eagles." That is God's promise to us now.

We, too, stand perplexed that one who had faced death as often as did this one, who had defied death even though missing in action and crashed in airplanes, who loved life and family, who kept himself physically fit through the golf he enjoyed, could be struck down by this disease at this age. But in our perplexity and pain, we look to God who gives strength.

He wore an eagle on his shoulder. God promises that as we wait on Him we can mount on eagles' wings to fly with faith. That those who wait on the Lord shall mount on eagles' wings implies that they fly higher. The most majestic of birds, the eagle, flies higher than other birds.

This man was a competitor. He had big goals, and he always moved toward them. As a Boy Scout, he was an Eagle Scout. As an Air Force officer, he wore an eagle; he was a colonel. He flew very high. As a boy, he wore an eagle on his breast. As a man, he wore an eagle on his shoulder. At his death, we are borne on eagles' wings.

God promises that we can fly higher yet with Him. He transports us into His very presence. Listen to His promise in John 14:1-3:

> Let not your hearts be troubled; believe in God, believe also in me. In my Father's house are many rooms; if it were not so, would I have told you that I go to prepare a place for you? And when I go and prepare a place for you, I will come again and will take you to myself, that where I am you may be also.

On eagles' wings implies that those who wait on the Lord shall see farther. From exalted heights one can see long distances. The Christian can see into eternity. He sees past the present sorrow into eternity. He sees past the pain and disability into eternity. He sees past the separation from loved ones into eternity and union with the one who loves us. Eternity is in the eyes because Christ is in the heart. Height gives perspective. Christians have perspective for life—and death.

On eagles' wings implies that those who

wait on the Lord shall stay longer. *Wait* has
a root meaning of "twist, bind, as in a
rope." We are bound to God.

Our friend lived longer than expected in
his case. Due to the power of God and the
exchange of strength, the Christian has the
power to exist to the very end—past time to
eternity.

And I think of another promise to God
which is also a confession of faith that men-
tions eagles' wings—Exodus 19:3-4:

> And Moses went up unto God, and the
> Lord called him out of the mountain, say-
> ing, "Thus shalt thou say to the house of
> Jacob, and tell the children of Israel: You
> have seen what I did unto the Egyptians,
> and how I bore you on eagles' wings, and
> brought you unto myself."

God strengthens. Faith enables Him to
work in our lives.

I thought of this Sunday night while sitting in the hospital room at the Air Force
base hospital, watching him struggle for
each breath with his tremendous will to
live. Then I shared it with his wife on the
morning of his death.

When you think of someone who is the
picture of a pilot, you think of someone who
looked like this man: eyes that had squinted
into the sun; face that had felt the wind; tall,
slim, a strong-looking man. He looked like
a flier.

And when you think of someone who
should look like a man from Canyon,
Texas, you think of someone who looked

like this man: tall, lean, eyes that squinted into the western sun, a face that had felt the wind; tough, but not rough; strong, but not overbearing; able, but gentle and loving, particularly to his family. He looked like a man who could mount his horse and ride into the sunset.

This makes you think of a person who makes virtues out of such things as love, faith, duty, honor, and country. That made me think of another military man who mentioned these on May 12, 1962, in his response to receiving the Thayer Award at the United States Military Academy at West Point. In his last speech to the "long, gray, line," General Douglas MacArthur said:

> Duty-Honor-Country. Those three hallowed words reverently dictate what you ought to be, what you can be, and what you will be. They are your rallying points: To build courage when courage seems to fail; to regain faith when there seems to be little cause for faith; to create hope when hope seems forlorn.

14
When the Savior Leads Us Like a Shepherd

He was the executive director of a national religious agency. His mother was in a nursing home far from where he worked and lived. He was visiting her over a weekend. When the Sunday morning worship time arrived, they watched a televised service together. She was long past attending the worship services as her lifetime custom had been.

One of the congregational hymns was "Savior Like a Shepherd Lead Us." That had always been one of her favorite hymns. She had not said much that was coherent that morning. Yet as the congregation sang the hymn, she joined in the singing, repeating practically every word of the hymn. The hymn had expressed one of her favorite and compelling thoughts: The Savior leads us like a shepherd.

The hymn is based on a favorite passage of Scripture, Psalm 23, the Shepherd Psalm. This well-known and well-loved psalm is especially meaningful at a time of sorrow due to the death of a loved one. We draw comfort from the thought that the Savior leads His people much as the shepherd would tenderly care for his sheep. When death casts its shadow over us, we are comforted by knowing that the Savior walks with us through the very valley of the shadow of death, protecting us as the shepherd would protect his sheep in a dangerous spot.

As Christians this is one of our greatest assurances: The Savior leads us like a shepherd. But what does it mean for the Savior to lead us like a shepherd?

When the Savior leads us like a shepherd we are aware of His *presence*. One of the things that strikes us about the twenty-third Psalm is the overpowering presence of the shepherd. Everything centers in the shepherd. Without the shepherd, there would be no reason for the expression of protective peace that runs through the psalm. We are much aware of God's presence in any time of sorrow. We can hardly think of facing a time of sorrow alone. The awareness of His presence is comforting, strengthening, and encouraging.

Notice, too, the personal nature of the presence of the shepherd. The psalmist said, "The Lord is *my* shepherd . . . he leads *me* [to green pastures]" (vv. 1-2, author's italics). Run through the psalm and note the use of the personal pronouns: I, me, mine. The expression of the personal nature of the shepherd's presence is throughout the psalm.

That is the kind of relationship we have with Christ. The personal relationship of faith allows us to profess Christ as Savior and to claim the Lord as our Shepherd. When the care, comfort, and control of our lives is needed (as these are needed in the experience of sheep), the Savior is there as a shepherd to provide them.

When the Savior leads us like a shepherd, we are aware of His *provision*. Notice the extent of the provisions for our care. In all of our needs, the Savior provides for us as a shepherd would provide for his sheep.

There is provision for physical needs. The shepherd leads to green pastures. In an arid climate, the time comes when the pastures grow brown and the grass dies. But the good shepherd knows where the pastures are green, growing, and lush. To those green pastures, the good shepherd leads his sheep. To the pools of still water, not the rushing torrents that could sweep the sheep away, the shepherd guides his sheep. In the quiet pools of water, they can quench their thirst. The Savior provides for physical needs.

But there is also a provision for emotional needs. He restores the soul. In those times when it seems that the soul is terribly disturbed, the mind is confused, and the heart is heavy, the good shepherd comes to quiet, to calm, to restore.

Provision is also made for spiritual needs. The Savior like a good shepherd leads into the paths of righteousness. We never find righteousness on our own. We only find it through the Savior's guidance. In accordance with His character—"for his name's sake"—He provides for our spiritual needs. God gives grace and strength.

Does our Savior have the resources for this kind of provision? In verse 5, the metaphor changes from that of a shepherd to an Oriental host. The host prepares a table from ample provisions. The cup he serves overflows with abundance. God has the resources for our care. He never runs short.

When the Savior leads us like a shepherd, we are aware of His *protection.* He protects us in the "valley of the shadow of death." If the sheep were walking through a narrow ravine and an eagle flew over them, with the shadow of the predator casting a shadow of death over the lamb which was his intended victim, the shepherd would protect them. And God protects us.

The Savior we serve and worship protects from evil. Evil is expressed in many ways, even in the ways that we might react in rebellion and bitterness toward death. But God protects us from that.

He protects from the enemies that would stalk us. The picture in verse 5 is that of a fleeing person entering a house of refuge. The host cared for him even though the enemies lurked outside. God gives us that protective care.

When the Savior leads us like a shepherd, we are aware of His *promise.* The promise is that God's goodness and mercy shall track our lives. At the time of the death of a loved one, we may think that sorrow and grief will follow us forever. God's promise is that we can know and experience His goodness and mercy in the time of sorrow and beyond.

The promise also holds out for us the assurance of eternal life in the Father's presence. "I shall dwell in the house of the Lord *forever*" (v. 6, author's italics) is the way the psalmist expressed it. The Savior expressed that promise in John 14.

Truly, the Savior leads us like a shepherd. That is one of our greatest assurances.

15
When God's
Peace Stands Guard

Although he did not identify himself, I have always suspected that the incident recorded by Ralph L. Herring in his book on Philippians, *Studies in Philippians,* was personal. Herring was the son of missionary parents. The incident concerned a boy who fled with his missionary parents before a revolutionary army in China. Their flight was on a train that had special permission to pass through the lines. He saw the opposing armies drawn up in battle array and the bullet scars on the buildings when they arrived in Hankow. That night the city was quiet. The fighting had passed further north. A contingent of British soldiers supported by a warship standing by on the Yangtze River had things under control. Outside his window was the measured tread of a British guard. He slept in peace.

The assurance of God's grace is that God's peace stands guard over our lives in times of danger, stress, and sorrow. Listen to Paul's expression of that truth to the Philippian Christians:

Be anxious for nothing, but in everything by prayer and supplication with thanksgiving let your requests be made known to God. And the peace of God, which sur-

passes all comprehension, shall guard
your hearts and your minds in Christ
Jesus (Phil. 4:6-7, NASB).

Notice that it is God's peace that stands
guard over our hearts and minds. Remember that Jesus promised us a kind of peace
that is different from the world's peace (see
John 14). This is the kind of peace that God
gives to us through Jesus Christ—a peace
that stands guard over our hearts and
minds.

In the face of the sorrow that you now
know, God's peace can stand guard over
your hearts and minds. Observe how God
does this for us.

When God's peace stands guard over our
hearts and minds, we have *security.* We seek
security in many ways. One of the ways in
which we seek security is through relationships. When a relationship is disrupted by
death, one emotion we feel is insecurity. A
person who meant so much to us, in whom
we trusted, and on whom we depended has
been taken from us. That makes us feel insecure.

But God stands before us to guard
our hearts and minds in Christ Jesus. That
is an assurance of security. In the face of
our insecurity, God's security is offered
through grace. The Bible assures us that of
all the things that can separate us from one
another not even death can separate us
from the love of God (Rom. 8:38-39).

Insecurity is often experienced because of
the uncertainty of the future without the

one who has died. All of our past may have been tied up in that person; and with the death of this individual, the future looks terribly uncertain.

But God also assures us of the future. Many of the promises to which we cling in times of sorrow are the promises that center in the future security through faith in God. The psalmist said with assurance, "And I will dwell in the house of the Lord forever" (Ps. 23:6, NASB). Jesus Himself affirmed, "In My Father's house are many dwelling places; if it were not so, I would have told you; for I go to prepare a place for you. And if I go and prepare a place for you, I will come again, and receive you to Myself; that where I am, there you may be also" (John 14:2-3, NASB). With our futures secure, the peace of God stands guard over our hearts and minds.

When God's peace stands guard over our hearts and minds, we experience *sufficiency*. Notice that the apostle began the passage with the admonition to be anxious for nothing. That is strong language for people who often are anxious over everything. Anxiety-ridden about what we will do next, about where we shall derive strength, about what life will be like for us now, we are made to realize that we do not have to worry at all. God is sufficient.

We have the testimony of the sufficiency of God's grace from the missionary apostle who suffered so many things, in so many ways, at so many times. He had prayed three times for God to remove the thorn from his flesh. Here is God's reply, "And He has said to me, 'My grace is sufficient for you, for power is perfected in weakness' " (2 Cor. 12:9, NASB). That is our assurance also: God's grace is sufficient for for our every need.

We may not always experience sufficiency. We may run out of time. We may run out of money. We may run out of patience or understanding. But we never run out of God's grace, God's strength, God's peace. That is always sufficient.

This becomes our prayer, the prayer for God's peace and presence, a supplication made with thanksgiving to the God who grants peace. The God who answers prayers will stand guard over our hearts and minds with peace.

When God's peace stands guard, we experience *salvation*. The Scripture expresses that the peace of God which stands guard over our hearts and minds is beyond comprehension. That is true in two ways. It may have to do with our own comprehension. We cannot comprehend how we can have such peace when we are in such sorrow. It just does not seem natural that the overwhelming feeling that we have is peace when there is turmoil in our hearts and confusion in our minds. Or it may have to do with the comprehension of others. Those around us simply cannot understand how we can have such peace when all they knew was grief in similar situations. But our promise is that God's peace stands guard over our hearts and minds. And we stand on that promise.

The reason? The reason is the salvation that we have known through faith in Jesus Christ. This letter was written to Christians. This promise was made to Christians. "In Christ Jesus" the peace of God is known. One of the results of salvation is peace. We have peace with God (Rom. 5:8). And we have peace from God.

God's peace stands guard over our hearts and minds in times of sorrow. That is our assurance. And that is our peace.

16
The Stewardship
of Sorrow

He was a professor in a seminary. His mother, a fine and faithful Christian woman, had been in a hospital at the point of death for two weeks. She died on a Wednesday evening. The call came just before our Wednesday evening prayer service began. After we had completed the prayer meeting, I left word that I was going to visit that professor and his family at their home.

Not long after I arrived, after we had discussed the death of his mother and the funeral arrangements and had prayer, the telephone rang. The call was for me. It was a message from my wife. Our pet dog had gotten out of the yard and had been run over. My daughter was particularly distraught because she had left the gate ajar and the dog had run out of the yard into the street where he had been run over. Immediately the people whom I had sought to comfort in their loss began to comfort me in our loss.

This is the stewardship of sorrow. Although the death of a pet dog cannot at all be compared with the death of a mother, the principle remains: We have a stewardship of sorrow. Having known sorrow and the strength that God gives in times of sorrow, we have a stewardship to provide comfort and strength to others.

We often need comfort. Particularly at a time of death we need comfort. The New Testament word that is translated *comfort* has as its root meaning brave or strong. The meaning of the word *comfort,* then, is "with strength" or "with bravery." With this in mind, we understand that the real meaning of comfort is more than soothing sympathy. Christian comfort brings courage, shares strength, and enables a person to cope with all that life has dealt or with all of which death has robbed.

How important is comfort? Listen to the words of Paul in the opening verses of his second letter to the Corinthian Christians:

> Blessed be the God and the Father of our Lord Jesus Christ, the Father of mercies and God of all comfort; who comforts us in all our affliction so that we may be able to comfort those who are in any affliction with the comfort with which we ourselves are comforted by God (1:3-4, NASB).

The comfort of God is so important that Paul used the same word five times in two verses. That was not because of a deficiency in his vocabulary or because of a limitation of literary expression. It was because of the importance of the comfort of God.

Running throughout that passage, too, is the expression of the stewardship of sorrow that we have. Each person who has been comforted by God in his or her affliction has a responsibility to share that comfort with others. Having known and experienced the comfort of God, Christians become comforting persons. These are persons who are qualified by their own experience to comfort others. They have known comfort; they give comfort. This stewardship is expressed to us by one who was no stranger to sorrow.

Consider, first, the *source* of our stewardship for sorrow. God is the source of our comfort. Paul called God "the Father of mercies and the God of comfort." What a beautifully expressive way to describe God! God can be described for us as the source of all the mercy and comfort which we receive in life.

The psalmist also expressed that when he said: "I will lift up my eyes to the mountains;/From whence does my help come?/ My help comes from the Lord,/Who made heaven and earth" (Ps. 121:1-2, NASB).

John, the seer, said in the Book of Revelation: "He [God] shall wipe away every tear from their eyes; and there shall no longer be any death; there shall no longer be any mourning, or crying, or pain" (21:4, NASB).

God is the source of our comfort. Our ultimate comfort comes from God. As with all gifts from God, we have the obligation to share that gift with others. That is our stewardship of sorrow: to share God's comfort with others.

Notice next the *scope* of our stewardship of sorrow. Nothing is omitted. The scope of our stewardship in sharing God's comfort extends to all the areas of human hurt and pain. It especially extends to sorrow from death.

According to the passage of Scripture written to the Corinthians, God comforts us in "all our afflictions." And we are to comfort others "in any affliction." That is, indeed, a wide scope of concern. God's love is broad enough to include us all and deep enough to care for all of our concerns.

In expressing God's comfort, do not fall into too easy a use of the will of God. God's ultimate will for each of us would be for us to have health and happiness. As our Father, God desires the very best for each of us. But we are humans and sometimes make bad choices. We live in community, so we are often the victims of other people's actions. While God could control all human actions, we are people and not puppets. Some things happen that are not what God would desire for us. God does not always explain. He does, however, always comfort.

Think, too, of the *strength* of the stewardship of sorrow. The strength comes from the added strength derived from comforting others and the strength that is given to others. Strength in the comforting of sorrow works in two directions: to the person who receives comfort and to the person who gives comfort.

We know the extent of God's strength by the comfort he gives in situations that we would all but consider comfortless. That strength is shared with others. In comforting others through our experience of the comfort of God, we share our strength with them as God has shared His strength with us. It is an act of strength.

Lord Byron said, "The drying up of a single tear has more/Of honest fame than shedding seas of gore."

There is stewardship of sorrow. We need to practice it as we have experienced it.

PART IV
A Word for You

17
When a Child Dies

I remember well the first funeral service I conducted for a child. He was a chubby, red-cheeked, blond-headed two-year-old. I had a chubby, red-cheeked, blond-headed two-year-old boy. They kept the casket open throughout the service. Every time I looked down at that casket I could not help but think more of my son than of their son. That funeral service was difficult, not only for the grieving family but also for the officiating minister.

The death of a child is always difficult. There is so much hope, promise, and potential represented in every child born into the world. Even though death always confronts us as an invader, it is more so when a child dies.

How do you explain death in these circumstances? A way we often explain it is by saying that the child has gone to be with Jesus. While that expression needs to be used with care so that other children do not get the impression that Jesus gathers up children in death, it is an adequate expression. The touch of Jesus is the touch of life and not of death. Christ gives life; He does not bring death.

You must be honest in your expressions also. While it is a tender thought that God now has another angel in heaven, that is not biblically correct. Angels are different created beings who serve God. Children are human beings, and human beings do not turn into angels.

A beautiful passage of Scripture tells us that Jesus is interested in little children and that He receives the little children who come to Him:

> And they were bringing children to Him so that He might touch them, and the disciples rebuked them. But when Jesus saw this, He was indignant and said to them, "Permit the children to come to Me; do not hinder them; for the kingdom of God belongs to such as these. Truly I say to you, whoever does not receive the kingdom of God like a child shall not enter it at all." And He took them in His arms and began blessing them, laying His hands upon them (Mark 10:13-16, NASB).

At that time the disciples were interested in protecting Jesus, so they wanted to send the children away. Jesus, instead, showed the disciples that He was interested in the children and wanted the opportunity to bless them.

When a child goes to be with Jesus through death, we think of the *awareness* of Jesus. Jesus was aware of the children. He knew what they meant to their parents and what His blessing would mean.

Every child is a gift of God. We are aware of what that child meant: the anticipation of her birth . . . the expectations for his life.

Each child is a child of promise. Each child has enormous potential. Jesus is as aware of that as we are.

We tend to become aware of all of the good experiences the child will miss in growing up. But we must also be aware that the child will miss rejection, sorrow, heartache, hurt, loneliness, and sin. During all of the brief life of the child, he has been surrounded by love and care. Some children never know anything but love. Had that child lived to maturity he would have experienced a lot of life that was not love.

When by death a child goes to be with Jesus, we think of the *assurance* of Jesus. We are thrust to God at the time of the death of a child. From God we can receive the assurance we need.

From our belief in God, we have the assurance that the soul or life of the child is safe. We believe that those who have not reached the age where they arc personally accountable for their decisions are safe in the Savior. From our experience with Christ, we have the assurance that life is eternal. From our knowledge of the Scripture, we have the assurance of the comfort and sympathy of God himself.

Think of three of children's favorite religious expressions and see the assurance they give.

A favorite song of children is "Jesus Loves Me." This gives us the assurance of God's love at all times. It is a love that is abiding. We cannot be separated from that love even by death.

A favorite mealtime prayer of children begins with the words, "God is great, God is good." This assures us of the goodness, grace, and mercy of God.

Before a child goes to bed at night, often the prayer is "Now I lay me down to sleep, I pray the Lord my soul to keep. And if I die before I wake, I pray the Lord my soul to take." This assures us of the continual care of God.

When in death, a child goes to be with Jesus we think of the *answer* of Jesus. Jesus came to give God's answer to us. Chief among the answers we desire now is the answer to the question of why a child had to die at such an early age. To that we cannot give a sure answer, as we cannot answer why any person dies at any age or under any circumstances. But Jesus does give us some sure answers.

One of these answers is that God did not take this child. Beware of the loose and easy use of the will of God. God's perfect will is that each person reach the fullness of that person's potential. But we live in an imperfect world where there is disease and danger. To say that God took the child is not correct. To say that God allowed the child to die because of the disease and disability that are parts of the world in which we live would be more correct. It may have taken a miracle to have kept that child from dying.

Another answer is that Christ will not leave us comfortless. He has promised an eternal life. He has promised that those who have been separated by death shall be reunited by faith. King David had a child to die. He expressed the faith that there would be a time of reunion with the child who was lost by death (2 Sam. 12:18-23).

A child has gone to be with Jesus. We experience sorrow, loss, and pain. But we also have hope and assurance because we believe in God.

18
When an Older
Person Dies

My Grandfather Carter lacked only one
week being ninety-eight years of age when
he died. His father-in-law, my great-grand-
father, died at the age of ninety-six. Without doubt, these would qualify as older
persons at the time of their deaths.

For the first time, the majority of the
citizens in the United States is older than
fifty years of age. There are more middle-
agers than teenagers. With the increased
longevity, more people will die at an older
age.

At whatever age death comes, we are
never quite ready for it. We are never ready
to die. Neither are we ever ready for one of
our loved ones to die. We can be very well
aware of the pain, the suffering, the loss of
vitality, and the curtailment of activities
that have befallen particular persons. But
when we get right down to it, we are still
not ready for them to die. But die they will.
And die we all will. Death is a part of life.
All things that live must at some time die.

For some, death comes at a full age.
After a lifetime of joy and sorrow, of work
and rest, of giving and receiving, death
comes.

Listen to this word of Eliphaz, one of
Job's comforters or counselors, in his at-

tempt to comfort Job in his time of intense suffering. "Thou shalt come to thy grave in a full age, like as a shock of corn cometh in his season" (Job 5:26). He was trying to give reassurance to Job that his sufferings at that time would not result in his death. He would come to death at a full age. Just as the shock of corn was stacked in the harvest season, Job would live out his life fully and not die until it was time.

These words of intended comfort also give reassurance to us. When one has lived a long life and has lived that life well, death comes as the full completion of that life. The seed of corn that is planted in the ground does not reach its full purpose until it has come to complete ripeness. It is then harvested. Its purpose has been realized. And so it is when death comes at a full age. Life is brought to its natural conclusion.

When death comes at a full age, a person has had plenty of time for *service*. The person who has lived out his or her life has had the opportunity to serve during that lifetime. For some people their whole lives are lives of service. They have devoted themselves to their families, or their communities, or their churches. Some people have dedicated themselves to their work to the extent that it is hardly possible to separate them from the service rendered to others.

We think, also, of the service of God. God is near to such persons because the fellowship and communion with God has been long and deep. God has spoken. And they have responded.

When life has been spent in service to others, it is never wasted. No matter that the name may not be recorded among the great of the world. If that life has been lived fully, unselfishly, servingly, those who survive do not have to apologize for the person.

When death comes at a full age, there is plenty of time for *salvation.* God gives us many opportunities to respond in faith to Him. An aged person has had the opportunity to make that commitment of faith.

This person has also had the opportunity to express that faith to others. The life can be lived in witness of God's grace. It can show the strength of the Christian faith throughout the trials of life. It can express the power of God to work in one's life over the long haul. For an older person who has spent years as a child of God, faith for the long term is demonstrated. A relationship with God is not just a short-term proposition. The person who has lived a long life of faithfulness has made that known.

The man was aged. He could hardly see. He could not hear a conversation held in a normal tone of voice. He walked with hesitation and difficulty. Yet every Sunday he walked to Sunday School and worship services with his well-worn Bible under his arm. When someone asked him why he took the time to come to church when he could not hear much that was happening and could not join in the services himself, he replied by saying that he just wanted people to know whose side he was on.

When a person has lived to an old age

with an active faith in God, that person has had an opportunity over a long period of time to show whose side he or she is on.

Death at a full age gives plenty of time for *strength*. That person had the opportunity over a long period of time to share strength with others. Older people have a resiliency born out of the years of life experiences with its sorrows and joys, its expectedness and its unexpectedness. From that they have derived strength which they share with others.

They have experienced their own strength too. They have shown strength in surviving long past the time others may have expected them to die.

Increasingly the death may come from cancer. But what is cancer's real strength when pitted against human strength? Or, greater than that, divine strength? From some anonymous source, I picked up this statement:

> Can cancer conquer you? I doubt
>   it . . . for
> cancer is so limited . . .
> It cannot cripple love,
> It cannot shatter hope,
> It cannot corrode faith,
> It cannot eat away peace,
> It cannot destroy confidence,
> It cannot kill friendship,
> It cannot shut out memories,
> It cannot silence courage,
> It cannot invade the soul,
> It cannot reduce eternal life,
> It cannot quench the Spirit,

It cannot lessen the power of the resurrection.

She was one of those strong Christian women who had lived to a full age. At her death, her daughter found a Scripture passage cut out and stuck on the wall, "In quietness and confidence is our strength." That pretty well expresses it.

19
When a Mate Dies

I had not seen him for some months after the funeral service for his wife. I had always thought of him as a very strong, self-sufficient sort of person. But that day he looked haggard. His face had a look of deep sadness about it. He moved as one in a fog. In our conversation, he said, "You just do not know what its like when you lose your mate of so many years."

I will confess that I do not know what it is like to lose a mate by death. Fortunately that is an experience that I have not had. But I have known many other people who have had that experience. And I have had the opportunity of observing other people when they have lost a mate. It is a wrenching experience. It does terribly disrupt life. It does throw one into deep grief.

All of life has to be rearranged upon the death of a mate. That mate may have been one upon which the other depended. Not only is there the emotional dependence that is involved but also, in the case of a wife who does not work outside the home, it may mean that the source of financial dependence has been removed. In the case of a husband who has assumed none of the responsibilities around the home, it may mean that the one upon whom he had depended for his meals, for the maintenance of his home, for the handling of the daily business matters for the family has been removed. He may be at a total loss in caring for his home, in providing for his meals, in understanding the family finances. If the family is young and dependent children are at home without a parent upon whom they depended, there are other problems. When one has depended very heavily on another person, the death of that person makes a big difference.

Because life has been rearranged so completely, some people may react too quickly. Without thoroughly thinking through their actions, they may make some decision that they will regret later. A man left with small children at the death of his wife may enter into marriage again too quickly. A woman whose husband died may start keeping company with someone else of uncertain character or take to drinking alcohol which she had not done previously. The decision may be made too soon to sell the house or to dispose of the business or to relocate. Hasty decisions can bring about regrets later. While in the depths of grief is not the best time to make a life-changing decision.

One must deal with the loneliness. When a companion is no longer present to share life, a person gets lonely. Other members of the family may still be at home, perhaps children who need care and certainly provide company, but this does not dispel the loneliness. A man whose wife had died in her mid-thirties explained his action in marrying again within two months by saying, "People say that it has only been forty-five days since she died. They forget that there have been forty-five nights also." He had trouble coping with the loneliness. And he was certainly not alone in that.

Many people will rally around at the time of death. Friends will call. Food will be sent. Messages of comfort and shared strength will be delivered. But what happens after the flowers fade? Those are the times when someone who has lost a mate needs the most help.

I knew a retired man who was very much a handyman. He helped a group of widows in the church with routine matters of maintenance in their homes. His wife usually went with him to visit while he made minor home repairs. He made sure that the furnace was operating when cold weather came, and even kept the yards, in some cases. Another couple I know has been very thoughtful to take a neighboring widow with them to the evening worship services of their church. People who are hesitant to return to an empty house or apartment in the evening can be helped by such thoughtful gestures.

After the death of a mate, a person often feels like a fifth wheel. Many activities are arranged for couples so that a widow or widower feels left out when she or he is no longer part of a couple. But why do all dinner parties have to have an even number of guests? An artificial arrangement of people just to have the same number of couples may be awkward. Each surviving person would like to be treated as a person. That person still has dignity, worth, and the fullness of personhood. The things that other people do for them and with them with their own personhood in mind are greatly appreciated.

People often wonder whether their departed mate can see them from heaven. Probably not. If heaven is a place of perfect peace, the knowledge of what is going on in this imperfect world would not necessarily be peaceful to them.

Jesus indicated that our primary relationship in heaven is of a higher type, a more spiritual, and if anything, a more intimate, relationship than on earth. We will probably know one another, but it will be in a different relationship. The Sadducees, who did not even believe in the resurrections, once tried to trip Jesus on the matter of the resurrection body (Matt. 22:23-33). They concocted a story about a woman who had married a man who died before they had any children. The Hebrews had a law, levirate marriage, which held that if a man died without a child to perpetuate his name, the man's brother would marry his widow. In this story the woman was married to seven brothers in succession before she died. The question they asked was whose wife would she be in the resurrection. By His answer, Jesus indicated that our relationships will be different in heaven. While we will probably know one another there, the relationship will not be the same as on earth; we will not be on earth. The primary relationship is with Christ.

When one remarries after a mate dies, the new mate does not take the place of the other. No one can take the place of the other mate. That person's place is secure. No one else can be the father of her children or the wife of his youth or the one with whom the struggle to build the business was shared or the one who helped him through school. The new mate has a new place, his or her place in that life.

When a mate dies, life is certainly made different. But God's love is secure. His presence is assured. He comforts.

20
When Parents Die

As is so often the case, her parents lived in another state at the opposite end of the nation from where she lived. Both had been ill. Her mother, in fact, had been an invalid for years. Then her father developed cancer. He had spent most of his time and energy the last years of his life caring for his wife. But it had become a real question as to which one of them would die first. The daughter had always assumed that her father would outlive her mother. He did, but only by a month. The mother died, and the daughter left her home and job to go across the country for her mother's funeral. She stayed a while longer to see that her father's needs were met then returned home. Two weeks after her return, four weeks after her mother's death, her father died. When I visited her in her home the afternoon of her father's death, she described it as a "double whammy." Indeed, it was. It is difficult enough to accept and to process the death of one parent. For both parents to die in such a short period of time is tough to take.

At times, a parent will outlive all of his or her children. But this is not often the situation. In the normal course of life, since parents are by definition older than their children, usually the parents die before the children die. In the usual and expected experiences of life, most people will experience the death of a parent. And most people face the death of both their parents.

When both parents die, a person has to accept the fact of mortality. Often sons and daughters assume that their parents will always be around. True, intellectually most persons have accepted the fact that all persons die. But personally accepting it for one's own parents is often another matter. This is particularly true for persons who have been unusually dependent upon their parents. They just never face up to the fact that the day will come when their parents will not be around to share life, to enrich life, to guide them in life, or to bail them out of the situations into which they get themselves. The fact of a parent's death hits hard in those times.

People are often struck with guilt when the second parent dies. They feel guilty for not paying more attention to their parents. Or they feel guilty about having placed them in a nursing home. Or they feel guilty even about growing up and leaving home. It is as though they had abandoned their parents. And now they do not have their parents.

It gets worse if one starts playing the "what if " game. That is the game that goes, "what if " I had been with them at the time? or "what if " I had not allowed them to go to the nursing home and had continued to keep them in my home? or "what if " I had taken them into my home rather than allowing them to continue to live in their own home? or "what if" I had supervised the taking of their medicine? That game can go on endlessly. It is a dead-end game. It does not accomplish anything. It only adds to guilt and grief. In all probability death would have occurred no matter what you had done. Death is inevitable. It is a fact of life.

There is an old story about King Canute. While the tide was coming in, he caused his royal seat to be put on the shore. With all the majesty that he could muster he said to the sea, "Thou sea, I charge thee come no further upon my Land, neither presume to wet the Feet of Thy Sovereign Lord." But the sea came rolling in as before and without reverence for his words washed upon him and got him wet. The king then arose and pointed out to the court flatterers the weak and frivolous powers of a king. We may need to be reminded of the power of death. We cannot stop it. We cannot keep it from coming. And all the "what ifs" in the world will not change the situation at all.

One should not feel guilty about feeling relieved when death comes to take the aged parent who has suffered a disabling disease or, if nothing else, the ravages of old age. For that person death may come more as a friend than as an enemy. She has lived her life. She has made her contribution. She has been a faithful and committed Christian. She has seen the goals of life met. And she has suffered enough. For that parent death is a relief. The suffering, pain, and disabilities are now over. Even if she had recovered she could never have known life as she had known and enjoyed it before. Do not feel guilty at feeling relieved. She has moved on to the next stage.

We have some assurances that we keep in mind each time we lose a parent through death. We have the assurance that we leave in the cemetery only the body that the individual occupied in the days of earthly life. We even call them the remains. The Scripture reminds us that we came from dust and to dust we will return. We have the assurance that the soul, the self, the person, has gone on to the God who gave life, who gives new life through faith in Jesus Christ, and who promises eternal life to us.

We have the assurance, also, that as Jesus Christ was resurrected from the dead so shall those who believe in him also be resurrected to live eternally with him. Listen to the words of the apostle Paul:

> For since we believe that Jesus died and rose again, even so, through Jesus, God will bring with him those who have fallen asleep. For the Lord himself will descend from heaven with a cry of command, with the archangel's call, and with the sound of the trumpet of God. And the dead in Christ will rise first; then we who are alive, who are left, shall be caught up together with them in the clouds to meet the Lord in the air; and so we shall always be with the Lord (1 Thess. 4:14, 16-17).

We thus have the assurance of resurrection and eternal life.

We have the assurance, too, that we do not leave that cemetery alone or comfortless. Jesus Himself said, "Lo, I am with you alway, even unto the end" (Matt. 28:20, KJV).

And what as we face the final foe? "Therefore comfort one another with these words" (1 Thess. 4:18). God gives us words of comfort, strength, and hope. Rely on them and trust Him.